★ *Voices from the Civil War* ★

WOMEN
& FAMILIES

edited by Tom Head

BLACKBIRCH®
PRESS

THOMSON
———★———
GALE

San Diego • Detroit • New York • San Francisco • Cleveland
New Haven, Conn. • Waterville, Maine • London • Munich

THOMSON

GALE

LIBRARY OF CONGRESS CATALOGING-IN-PUBLICATION DATA

Head, Tom,
  Women and families / [compiled] by Tom Head.
    p. cm. — (Voices from the Civil War)
  Includes bibliographical references (p. 31) and index.
  ISBN 1-56711-797-X (lib. bdg. : alk. paper)
  1. United states—History—Civil War, 1861-1865—Women. 2. United States—History—Civil War, 1861-1865—Children. 3. United States—History—Civil War, 1861-1865—Personal Narratives. 4. Women—United states—Biography. 5. Children—United States—Biography. I. Head, Tom. II. Series.

E625 .W65 2003
973.7'81—dc21

2002027795

Printed in United States
10 9 8 7 6 5 4 3 2 1

Contents

★ *Introduction* ★

CIVILIANS IN THE CIVIL WAR

B eginning in 1861, the American Civil War tore the nation apart. Millions of American men joined the ranks of the Union and Confederate armies and fought across the country's vast landscapes. The war was not, however, only a soldier's fight. As armies clashed in Virginia, Tennessee, Pennsylvania, and other states, the civilians who lived in these regions were drawn into the war. Homes were turned into hospitals, prisons, or military barracks. Leaders on both sides deliberately attacked civilians and their property in an attempt to win the war. Civilian women and families of the Civil War were more directly involved in the conflict than American civilians in any war before or since.

The Civil War was also the first major American conflict in which a significant number of women played an active role. An estimated four hundred women actually entered combat. Civilian women also contributed to the war as nurses, spies, and antislavery activists.

More than five thousand women served as nurses during the Civil War. Most were unpaid volunteers. Union nurses generally served in field hospitals and were under the supervision of a national organization that sent them along with Union armies as they were needed. Soldiers who required further treatment were transferred to larger hospitals that were also staffed by women nurses. Confederate nurses did not have access to the sort of support and organization Union nurses had. Southern nurses did the best they could and adapted houses into makeshift hospitals. Nurses on both sides faced weeks of relative calm, followed by one-day battles that resulted in thousands of severely injured soldiers.

Medical knowledge in the Civil War era was not very advanced by modern standards. A severe battle injury that did not heal on its own, and could not be corrected

---

American women played a greater part in the Civil War than in any other American war. Most volunteered as nurses, as depicted in this drawing.

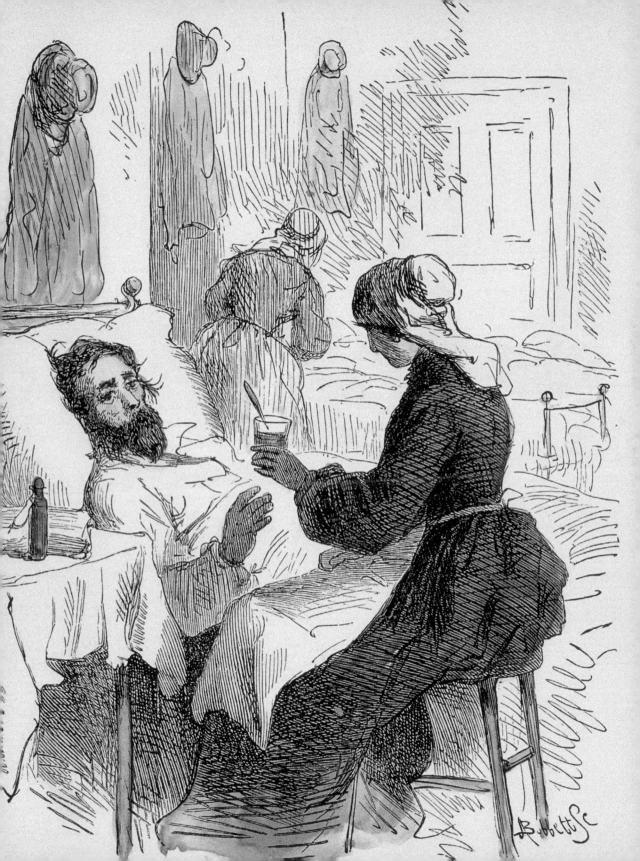

by amputating a limb, could easily result in death. Battle wounds were not the only problem. Of the 620,000 soldiers who died in the Civil War, about two-thirds died of disease. Smallpox and tuberculosis were fairly common and difficult to treat. Nurses taught soldiers proper hygiene to reduce outbreaks, and treated those affected as best they could.

There is no reliable estimate of the number of women who served as spies during the Civil War. One of the most famous spies was Emmeline Piggott. She smuggled notes for the Confederacy by pinning them to her skirt. Union spy Pauline Cushman, an actress, sometimes assumed false identities to get information from Confederates. Confederate spy Belle Boyd once raced across an active battle-field to warn of an impending Union attack.

Some of the most influential antislavery activists of the Civil War era were also women. Sojourner Truth was one of the most vocal and well-known feminists of her time. Truth was also a former slave who had worked as an abolitionist. Susan B. Anthony and Elizabeth Cady Stanton, who had dedicated most of their lives to women's suffrage (the right to vote), turned their attention to the abolition of slavery when war broke out. Stanton and Anthony helped to start what became a large-scale civil rights movement after the war. Former slave Harriet Tubman risked her life to make nineteen trips to the South to help slaves escape north using the Underground Railroad (an informal network of abolitionists who led slaves away from captivity).

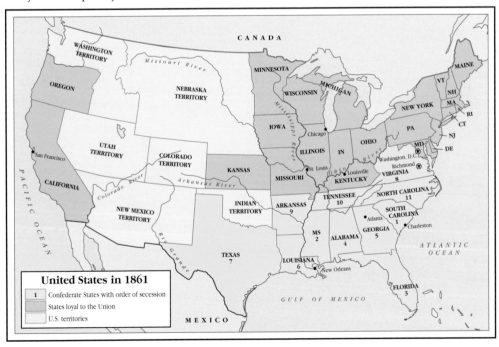

It is from women that historians have pieced together the most detailed civilian accounts of the war. Southerner Mary Chesnut, wife of a U.S. senator from South Carolina, wrote an extensive diary that provides insights into the motives of the Southern rebels. Women on both sides documented the greatest atrocities of the war. These include Union general William T. Sherman's burning of Atlanta, Confederate general Jubal Early's attacks on Washington and Pennsylvania, and the dismal lives that people were forced to lead when their cities faced daily bombardment.

Children were also forced to play an active role in the Civil War. At least 325 children aged thirteen and under actually served on the battlefield. Those who remained at home faced increased responsibilities. They worked full-time jobs, planted crops, and sometimes repaired war

A former slave and one of the foremost feminists of her time, Sojourner Truth (pictured) wrote and lectured on women's rights and the abolition of slavery.

damage. Like other free civilians who did not fight in the war, women and children were forced to keep American society functioning as well as it could during the desperate years of warfare.

★ Chronology of the Civil War ★

November 1860   **December 1860–March 1861**   **April 1861**

Abraham Lincoln is elected president of the United States.

• Concerned about Lincoln's policy against slavery in the West, the South Carolina legislature unanimously votes to secede from the United States. Alabama, Florida, Georgia, Louisiana, Mississippi, and Texas secede from the Union, and form the Confederate States of America.

• Mississippi senator Jefferson Davis becomes president of the Confederacy.

• Arkansas, North Carolina, Tennessee, and Virginia later join the rebellion.

Confederate troops fire on Union-occupied Fort Sumter in South Carolina and force a surrender. This hostile act begins the Civil War.

September 1862–January 1863

• Lee's Army of Northern Virginia and George McClellan's Army of the Potomac fight the war's bloodiest one-day battle at Antietam, Maryland. Though the battle is a draw, Lee's forces retreat to Virginia.

• Abraham Lincoln issues the Emancipation Proclamation that declares all slaves in Confederate states to be forever free. Three months later it takes effect.

September 1864

Atlanta, Georgia, surrenders to Union general William T. Sherman, who orders Atlanta evacuated and then burned. Over the coming months, he begins his March to the Sea to Savannah. His troops destroy an estimated $100 million worth of civilian property in an attempt to cut rebel supply lines and reduce morale.

Jefferson Davis, president of the Confederate States of America

July 1861

Confederate troops defeat Union forces at the First Battle of Manassas (First Bull Run) in Fairfax County, Virginia, the first large-scale battle of the war.

April 1862

• Confederate troops are defeated at the Battle of Shiloh in Tennessee. An estimated 23,750 soldiers are killed, wounded, or missing, more than in all previous American wars combined.

• Slavery is officially abolished in the District of Columbia; the only Union slave states left are Delaware, Kentucky, Maryland, and Missouri.

June 1862

General Robert E. Lee assumes command of the Conferate Army of Northern Virginia.

Robert E. Lee

August 1862

Confederate troops defeat Union forces at the Second Battle of Manassas (Second Bull Run) in Prince William County, Virginia.

July 1863

Union forces stop the South's invasion of the North at Gettysburg, Pennsylvania. Lasting three days, it is the bloodiest battle of the war.

November 1863

President Abraham Lincoln delivers the Gettysburg Address in honor of those who died at the war's bloodiest battle at Gettysburg.

April 1865

• Confederate general Robert E. Lee surrenders to Union general Ulysses S. Grant. This ends the Civil War on April 9.

• Five days later, President Lincoln is assassinated by actor John Wilkes Booth.

December 1865

The Thirteenth Amendment becomes law and abolishes slavery in the United States.

Abraham Lincoln, president of the United States of America

★ Mary Black Ford ★
REPORTING ON SLAVERY

Women played a major role as journalists before and after the Civil War. As they recorded daily life before and during the war, these women took note of injustice wherever they encountered it. In this excerpt from her Notes Illustrative of the Wrongs of Slavery *(1832), Virginia abolitionist reporter Mary Black Ford describes two incidents that highlighted the injustice of slavery. Reports by Ford and other authors helped spread abolitionist feelings in the North. This convinced many to fight to end slavery in America during the war.*

● **Mary Black Ford,** *Notes Illustrative of the Wrongs of Slavery*, **1832.**

Directly across the street from our house in Fredericksburg lives a Negro trader of the name of Finnall. Last summer a young negro man was sold to him who was strongly suspected of the crime of wishing to make his escape to one of the Free States. So his Mistress sold him to this Trader, who confined him in his cellar, not having a jail at hand then. The Mother of this young man was an old woman whom I knew, an excellent and pious woman. This was her only son, her greatest earthly comfort. She would often come to visit him in his cellar. . . . When the time drew near for them all to be driven South, the Mother came to the house and very earnestly solicited the young man who had charge of them (the Trader being away), to permit her to see him once more. This was refused. . . .

Finnall, the Negro trader who lives diagonally opposite to us, set off with a large gang of Slaves for the Southern Market. There were many women, girls and boys who set off from this place, the men coming afterwards. They are generally chained and handcuffed. Capt. Henry Philips, who lives very near us, has sold to go in this gang, a little girl twelve or thirteen years old, named Melinda. . . . She was a favorite with those who knew her. . . . The sale had been very sudden. The only reason given for selling her was that Mrs. Philips said she could do her own work. I saw the company of females weeping as they walked before the Drivers, stopping occasionally as they proceeded, to take leave of their friends and relatives as they met them.

Think what it is to be a Slave!!! To be treated not as a Man, but as . . . a thing that may be bought and sold, to have no right to the fruits of your own labour, no right to your own wife and children, liable at any moment to be separated at the arbitrary will of another from all that is dearest to you on earth, and whom it is your duty to love and cherish. . . . Think of this, and all the nameless horrors that are concentrated in that one word Slavery.

GLOSSARY
- **Negro trader:** slave trader
- **Free States:** Northern states where slavery had been abolished
- **pious:** religious
- **solicited:** asked
- **arbitrary:** unjustified

★ Mary Chesnut ★

AN ANXIOUS SOUTH

When the Civil War began, many people in the North and the South expected the fighting to end quickly. By June 1861 there had been no large-scale battle, and many Southerners lived in fear of a Union attack. Mary Chesnut, the wife of a U.S. senator from South Carolina, was well educated and familiar with the political climate of the time. Her Diary from Dixie, *published twenty years after her death, is probably the most widely read civilian account of the Civil War. In this June 24 entry from her diary, Chesnut describes the tension many civilians felt in the early days of war.*

• **Mary Chesnut,** *Diary from Dixie.* **New York: Appleton, 1905.**

L ast night I was awakened by loud talking and candles flashing, tramping of feet, growls dying away in the distance, loud calls from point to point in the yard. Up I started, my heart in my mouth. Some dreadful thing had happened, a battle, a death, a horrible accident. Some one was screaming aloft—that is, from the top of the stairway, hoarsely like a boatswain in a storm. Old Colonel Chesnut was storming at the sleepy negroes looking for fire, with lighted candles, in closets and everywhere else. I dressed and came upon the scene of action.

"What is it? Any news?" "No, no, only mamma smells a smell; she thinks something is burning somewhere." The whole yard was alive, literally swarming. There are sixty or seventy people kept here to wait upon this household, two-thirds of them too old or too young to be of any use, but families remain intact. The old Colonel has a magnificent voice. I am sure it can be heard for miles. Literally, he was roaring from the piazza, giving orders to the busy crowd who were hunting the smell of fire.

Old Mrs. Chesnut is deaf; so she did not know what a commotion she was creating. She is very sensitive to bad odors. Candles have to be taken out of the room to be snuffed. Lamps are extinguished only in the porticoes, or farther afield. She finds violets oppressive, can only tolerate a single kind of sweet rose. A tea-rose she will not have in her room. She was totally innocent of the storm she had raised, and in a mild, sweet voice was suggesting places to be searched. I was weak enough to laugh hysterically. The bombardment of Fort Sumter was nothing to this.

After this alarm, enough to wake the dead, the smell was found. A family had been boiling soap. Around the soap-pot they had swept up some woolen rags. Raking up the fire to make all safe before going to bed, this was heaped up with the ashes, and its faint smoldering tainted the air, at least to Mrs. Chesnut's nose, two hundred yards or more away.

> **GLOSSARY**
> - **boatswain:** sailor
> - **piazza:** porch
> - **porticoes:** covered entrances to a building
> - **smoldering:** burning slowly

★ *Rose O'Neal Greenhow* ★

LETTER FROM PRISON

When the Southern states began to secede from the Union in 1860, Rose O'Neal Greenhow strongly supported the Confederate cause to become a separate nation. She became a spy for the South during the Civil War. Greenhow was considered to be one of the best. She carried an important message to P.G.T. Beauregard and is credited with helping him win at the Battle of Bull Run. In 1861, Rose O'Neal Greenhow was arrested by Union officials. While in prison, Greenhow wrote a letter to the U.S. secretary of state, William H. Seward. In the letter, she demanded an explanation for her arrest. She also warned Seward that no efforts by the Union army would stop the Southern resistance. The letter was printed in the Southern newspaper, the Richmond Whig, *and caused a great deal of controversy. Rose O'Neal Greenhow drowned in a boating accident in 1864. When her boat capsized, she was weighed down by gold in her pockets that she had earned from a book sale. Greenhow was buried with the Confederate flag, and the inscription on her tombstone read, "Mrs. Rose O'N. Greenhow, a bearer of dispatchs [sic] to the Confederate Government."*

- **Rose O'Neal Greenhow, "Letter to Honorable William H. Seward,"** ***Richmond Whig, 1861.***

Washington, Nov. 17th, 1861
To the Hon. Wm. H. Seward, Secretary of State:
Sir—For nearly three months I have been confined, a close prisoner, shut out from air and exercise, and denied all communication with family and friends.

I therefore most respectfully submit, that on Friday, August 23d, without warrant or other show of authority, I was arrested by the Detective Police, and my house taken in charge by them; that all my private letters, and my papers of a life time, were read and examined by them; that every law of decency was violated in the search of my house and person, and the surveilance . . . over me.

…And thus for a period of seven days, I, with my little child, was placed absolutely at the mercy of men without character or responsibility; that during the first evening, a portion of these men became brutally drunk, and boasted in my hearing of the "nice times" they expected to have with the female prisoners; and that rude violence was used towards a colored servant girl during that evening, the extent of which I have not been able to learn.

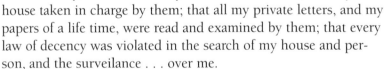

GLOSSARY

- **confined:** put in prison
- **warrant:** good reason
- **surveilance:** watching
- **ken:** knowledge
- **digression:** departure from the main point

Rose O'Neal Greenhow (pictured, right) served the Confederate cause as a spy during the Civil War.

You have held me, sir, to man's accountability, and I therefore claim the right to speak on subjects usually considered beyound a woman's ken, and which you may class as "errors of opinion." I offer no excuse for this long digression, as a three months' imprisonment, without formula of law, gives me authority for occupying even the precious moments of a Secretary of State.

The "iron heel of power" may keep down, but it cannot crush out, the spirit of resistance in a people armed for the defence of their rights; and I tell you now, sir, that you are standing over a crater, whose smothered fires in a moment may burst forth.

In conclusion, I respectfully ask your attention to this protest,
(Signed)
Rose O' N. Greenhow

★ *Theodore F. Upson* ★
NEWS OF THE COMING WAR

The Civil War began in April 1861, when Confederate troops took control of Fort Sumter in South Carolina. Immediately, millions of men both Northern and Southern were forced to choose between service to their home states and service to their country. In this excerpt from his journal, fifteen-year-old Theodore F. Upson reacts to the news of war. Upson later joined the Union army, and served until the end of the war.

- **Theodore F. Upson, *With Sherman to the Sea: The Civil War Letters, Diaries, and Reminiscences of Theodore F. Upson.* Baton Rouge: Louisiana State University Press, 1943.**

Father and I were husking out some corn. . . . When William Cory came across the field (he had been down after the mail) he was excited and said, "Jonathan the Rebs have fired upon and taken Fort Sumpter [*sic*]." Father got white and couldn't say a word.

William said, "The President will fix them. He has called for 75,000 men and is going to blocade their ports, and just as soon as those fellows find out that the North means business they will get down off their high horse."

Father said little. We did not finish the crop and drove to the barn. Father left me to unload and put out the team [of horses] and went to the house. After I had finished I went in to dinner. Mother said, "What is the matter with Father?" He had gone right upstairs. I told her what we had heard. She went to him. After a while they came down. Father looked ten years older.

We sat down to the table. Grandma wanted to know what was the trouble. Father told her and she began to cry. "Oh my poor children in the South! Now they will suffer! God knows how they will suffer! I knew it would come! Jonathan I told you it would come!"

"They can come here and stay," said Father.

"No they will not do that. [The South] is their home. There they will stay. Oh to think that I should have lived to see the day when Brother should rise against Brother."

She and mother were crying and I lit out for the barn. I do hate to see women cry.

We had another meeting at the school house last night; we are raising money to take care of the families of those who enlist. A good many gave money, others subscribed. The Hulper boys have enlisted and Steve Lampman and some others. I said I would go

GLOSSARY

- **Rebs:** Rebels (Confederates)
- **blocade:** blockade
- **subscribed:** agreed in advance to give money later
- **galop:** gallop
- **mullin:** a type of plant

Many men volunteered to go off and fight at the outbreak of the Civil War. This painting depicts a Union army colonel leading a unit of infantry volunteers.

but they laughed at me and said they wanted men not boys for this job; that it would all be over soon; that those fellows down South were big bluffers and would rather talk than fight. I am not so sure about that. I know the Hale boys would fight with [their] fists at any rate and I believe they would fight with guns too if needs be. I remember how Charlie [Hale] would get on our Dick [a horse] and ride on a galop across our south field cutting mullin heads with his wooden sword playing they were Indians or Mexicans (his father was in the Mexican War), and he looked fine. To be sure there was no danger but I feel pretty certain he could fight. May be it wont be such a picnic as some say it will. There has been a fight down in Virginia at Big Bethel. Al Beecher's Nephew was in it and wrote to his Uncle and he read the letter in his store. I could not make out which side whipped but from the papers I think the Rebels had the best of it. Mother had a letter from the Hales. Charlie and his Father are in [their] army and Dayton wanted to go but was too young. I wonder if I were in our army and they should meet me would they shoot me. I suppose they would.

★ Belle Boyd ★
A SPY FOR THE CONFEDERACY

Women played a vital role as spies for both the Union and Confederacy during the Civil War. Among the most well known Confederate spies was Belle Boyd. Her efforts at the Battle of Front Royal, Virginia, in May 1862 helped ensure a Confederate victory. Union troops had planned to destroy bridges in Front Royal in an attempt to divide the attacking Confederate forces. Boyd ran across the battlefield and warned Confederate troops to march into the town early. She hoped this would interrupt the Union plan. For her efforts, Confederate general Thomas "Stonewall" Jackson made Boyd an honorary captain. In this excerpt from her autobiography, Boyd describes her contribution to the Battle of Front Royal.

- **Belle Boyd, *Belle Boyd in Camp and Prison*. 2 volumes. London: Saunders, Otley & Co., 1865.**

I again went down to the door, and this time I observed, standing about in groups, several men who had always professed attachment to the cause of the South. I demanded if there was one among them who would venture to carry to General Jackson the information I possessed. They all with one accord said, "No, no. You go."

I did not stop to reflect. My heart, though beating fast, was not appalled. I put on a white sun-bonnet, and started at a run down the street, which was thronged with Federal officers and men. I soon cleared the town and gained the open fields, which I traversed with unabated speed, hoping to escape observation until such time as I could make good my way to the Confederate line, which was still rapidly advancing.

I had on a dark blue dress, with a little fancy white apron over it; and this contrast of colors, being visible at a great distance, made me far more conspicuous than was just then agreeable. The skirmishing between the outposts was sharp. . . .

My escape was most providential; for, although I was not hit, the rifle-balls flew thick and fast about me, and more than one struck the ground so near my feet as to throw the dust in my eyes. . . .

Upon this occasion my life was spared by what seemed to me then, and seems still, little short of a miracle; for, besides the numerous bullets that whistled by my ears, several actually pierced different parts of my clothing, but not one reached my body. Besides all this, I was exposed to a cross fire from the Federal and Confederate

GLOSSARY
- **appalled:** shocked
- **unabated:** unrestricted
- **Federal:** Union
- **conspicuous:** obvious
- **providential:** intended by God
- **career:** course
- **preternatural:** beyond ordinary
- **intimate:** indicate
- **approbation:** approval

Gen. Thomas "Stonewall" Jackson (on center horse) directed his troops at the Battle of Front Royal according to vital information brought by Belle Boyd.

artillery, whose shot and shell flew whistling and hissing over my head.

At length a Federal shell struck the ground within twenty yards of my feet; and the explosion, of course, sent the fragments flying, in every direction around me. I had, however, just time to throw myself flat upon the ground before the deadly engine burst; and again Providence spared my life.

Springing up when the danger was passed, I pursued my career, still under a heavy fire. I shall never run again as I ran on that, to me, memorable day. Hope, fear, the love of life, and the determination to serve my country to the last, conspired to fill my heart with more than feminine courage, and to lend preternatural strength and swiftness to my limbs. I often marvel and even shudder when I reflect how I cleared the fields and bounded over the fences with the agility of a deer.

Belle Boyd's war efforts earned her the rank of honorary captain in the Confederate army.

As I neared our line I waved my bonnet to our soldiers, to intimate that they should press forward, upon which one regiment, the 1st Maryland "rebel" Infantry, and Hay's Louisiana Brigade, gave me a loud cheer, and, without waiting for further orders, dashed upon the town at a rapid pace.

They did not then know who I was, and they were naturally surprised to see a woman on the battle-field, and on a spot, too, where the fire was so hot. Their shouts of approbation and triumph rang in my ears for many a day afterwards, and I still hear them not unfrequently in my dreams.

★ Louisa May Alcott ★
NURSING THE WOUNDED

Famed author Louisa May Alcott was a Civil War nurse.

In 1862, Louisa May Alcott was building a reputation as one of the most promising young writers in the United States. Her work was regularly featured in the largest magazines of the day. Her plays were also well received. Out of compassion and boredom, Alcott decided to leave her writing career behind for awhile and become a Union nurse. Alcott was forced to leave after only a month of work when she came down with typhoid. She wrote her Hospital Sketches *(which were based on letters she sent home to her family) during this time. They received very positive reviews and can be credited to some extent for pushing her writing career forward. Alcott went on to write thirty-five books, including* Little Women *(1868). In this excerpt from* Hospital Sketches, *Alcott describes her first day of work as a nurse. She had to respond to the wounded from the Battle of Fredericksburg.*

• **Louisa May Alcott,** *Hospital Sketches.* **Boston: Redpath, 1863.**

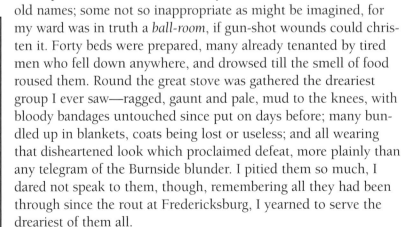

The sight of several stretchers, each with its legless, armless, or desperately wounded occupant, entering my ward, admonished me that I was there to work, not to wonder or weep; so I corked up my feelings, and returned to the path of duty, which was rather "a hard road to travel" just then. The house had been a hotel before hospitals were needed, and many of the doors still bore their old names; some not so inappropriate as might be imagined, for my ward was in truth a *ball-room*, if gun-shot wounds could christen it. Forty beds were prepared, many already tenanted by tired men who fell down anywhere, and drowsed till the smell of food roused them. Round the great stove was gathered the dreariest group I ever saw—ragged, gaunt and pale, mud to the knees, with bloody bandages untouched since put on days before; many bundled up in blankets, coats being lost or useless; and all wearing that disheartened look which proclaimed defeat, more plainly than any telegram of the Burnside blunder. I pitied them so much, I dared not speak to them, though, remembering all they had been through since the rout at Fredericksburg, I yearned to serve the dreariest of them all.

GLOSSARY
- **tenanted:** occupied
- **proclaimed:** announced
- **the Burnside blunder:** the loss at the Battle of Fredericksburg was blamed on Union general Ambrose Burnside.

★ Cornelia Peake McDonald ★
CHRISTMAS IN OCCUPIED VIRGINIA

During the Civil War, the town of Winchester, Virginia, was occupied and abandoned by Union soldiers seventy-two times. In this diary entry, Winchester housewife Cornelia Peake McDonald describes what Christmas Day, 1862, was like under strict Union occupation. One day after this entry was written, Union soldiers threatened to evict McDonald's family and convert their home into a hospital after her young son was overheard using the unflattering term "Yankees," to describe Union troops.

• **Cornelia Peake McDonald, *A Woman's Civil War.* Ed. by Minrose C. Gwin. Madison: University of Wisconsin Press, 1992.**

Some Southern plantation houses, like the one pictured here, were converted into Union army hospitals.

T he day has been too restless to enjoy, or even to realize that it was Christmas. All day reports of the advance of the Confederates. . . . Just as we were sitting down to dinner, we heard repeated reports of cannon. We hurried from the table and found the [Union] troops all hastily marching off. They expected a fight, I was told by one, as the Confederates were near town. We could eat no more dinner, the girls and myself, so it was carefully put away till we could enjoy it.

In the evening I went over to Mr. Woods' to see how the old people were bearing their burden, and to take them something nice from the dessert we could not eat. Found them all very quiet, but sad enough. The poor old gentleman's head looks whiter, and his forehead more wrinkled than before they [the Union soldiers] came to intrude on his sweet, quiet home.

GLOSSARY
• **reports:** firing sounds

★ Clara Barton ★

ON THE EVE OF A BLOODY BATTLE

In December 1862, Union troops struck at Robert E. Lee's Army of Northern Virginia in the city of Fredericksburg, Virginia. In their assault on Fredericksburg, Union troops had to cross rivers over portable bridges. These bridges were vulnerable to attack, which increased the likelihood of high Union casualties. As a Union nurse, Clara Barton was concerned about this possibility. She wrote to her cousin early in the morning on the second day of fighting. She feared immense pain and death would result from the battle. The Confederacy won the Battle of Fredericksburg. After several days of hard fighting, the Union troops were driven back over the portable bridges. The casualties were indeed high for the Union. Nearly five thousand soldiers were killed or wounded. The Confederacy, though, lost more than thirteen thousand soldiers. Clara Barton's role during the Civil War was legendary. Known as the "angel of the battlefield," she operated independently and served as a Union nurse whenever and wherever she felt she was most needed. After the war ended, she founded the American Red Cross.

• Clara Barton, Letter to Her Cousin, December 12, 1862.

My dear Cousin Vira:

Five minutes time with you; and God only knows what those five minutes might be worth to the many-doomed thousands sleeping around me.

It is the night before a battle. The enemy, Fredericksburg, and its mighty entrenchments lie before us, the river between—at tomorrow's dawn our troops will assay to cross, and the guns of the enemy will sweep those frail bridges at every breath.

The moon is shining through the soft haze with a brightness almost prophetic. For the last half hour I have stood alone in the awful stillness of its glimmering light gazing upon the strange sad scene around me striving to say, "Thy will Oh God be done."

The camp fires blaze with unwanted brightness, the sentry's tread is still but quick—the acres of little shelter tents are dark and still as death, no wonder for us as I gazed sorrowfully upon them. I thought I could almost hear the slow flap of the grim messenger's wings, as one by one he sought and selected his victims for the morning. Sleep weary one, sleep and rest for tomorrow toil. Oh! Sleep and visit in dreams once more the loved ones nestling at home. They may yet live to dream of you, cold lifeless and bloody, but this dream soldier is thy last, paint it brightly, dream it well. Oh northern mothers wives and sisters, all unconscious of the

GLOSSARY

- **entrenchments:** trenches
- **assay:** try
- **prophetic:** predicting the future
- **sentry:** guard
- **grim messenger:** death
- **unconscious:** unaware

**After the Civil War, Union volunteer nurse Clara Barton went on to found the
American Red Cross.**

hour, would to Heaven that I could bear for you the concentrated woe which is so
soon to follow, would that Christ would teach my soul a prayer that would plead to
the Father for grace sufficient for you, God pity and strengthen you every one.

Mine are not the only waking hours, the light yet burns brightly in our kind
hearted General's tent where he pens what may be a last farewell to his wife and
children and thinks sadly of his fated men.

Already the roll of the moving artillery is sounded in my ears. The battle draws
near and I must catch one hour's sleep for tomorrow's labor.

Good night near [dear] cousin and Heaven grant you strength for your more
peaceful and less terrible, but not less weary days than mine.

Yours in love, Clara

★ Susan B. Anthony and Elizabeth Cady Stanton ★

WOMEN'S RIGHTS AND THE ABOLITION OF SLAVERY

In the chaos of the Civil War, the women's suffrage (right to vote) movement collapsed. Meetings were canceled, and the most vocal members of the movement refocused their attention to end slavery. Among those concerned with the slavery issue was writer Elizabeth Cady Stanton. Stanton had been arguing for abolition long before the war began. She even spent her 1839 honeymoon at a European antislavery convention. Susan B. Anthony, on the other hand, wrote that she was "sick at heart" at the way the women's suffrage movement had gone silent during the war. Gradually, Stanton and Anthony came to an understanding shared by many at the time—that the abolition of slavery and women's suffrage were related issues. In March 1863, they published this joint statement calling for a national convention of loyal Northern women. This convention was dedicated to ending slavery and securing rights for women. The convention's first meeting took place later that year. It grew into a movement that favored total abolition, then full civil rights for former slaves. Stanton and Anthony lived to see the Fifteenth Amendment pass, guaranteeing men of all races the right to vote. Neither, though, lived to see the Nineteenth Amendment extend the same right to women in 1920.

- **Susan B. Anthony and Elizabeth Cady Stanton, "Call for a Meeting of the Loyal Women of the Nation," 1863.**

I n this crisis of our country's destiny, it is the duty of every citizen to consider the peculiar blessings of a republican form of government, and decide what sacrifices of wealth and life are demanded for its defence and preservation. The policy of the war, our whole future life, depends on a clearly-defined idea of the end proposed, and the immense advantages to be secured to ourselves and all mankind, by its accomplishment. No mere party or sectional cry, no technicalities of Constitution or military law, no mottoes of craft or policy are big enough to touch the great heart of a nation in the midst of revolution. A grand idea, such as freedom or justice, is needful to kindle and sustain the fires of a high enthusiasm.

At this hour, the best word and work of every man and woman are imperatively demanded. To man, by common consent, is

GLOSSARY
- **peculiar:** unique
- **sectional:** regional
- **imperatively:** with authority
- **counsel:** discussion

In 1863, Susan B. Anthony (left) and Elizabeth Cady Stanton (right) organized Northern women to fight for women's rights and the abolition of slavery.

assigned the forum, camp, and field. What is woman's legitimate work, and how she may best accomplish it, is worthy our earnest counsel one with another. We have heard many complaints of the lack of enthusiasm among Northern women; but, when a mother lays her son on the altar of her country, she asks an object equal to the sacrifice. In nursing the sick and wounded, knitting socks, scraping lint, and making jellies, the bravest and best may weary if the thoughts mount not in faith to something beyond and above it all. Work is worship only when a noble purpose fills the soul. Woman is equally interested and responsible with man in the final settlement of this problem of self-government; therefore let none stand idle spectators now. When every hour is big with destiny, and each delay but complicates our difficulties, it is high time for the daughters of the revolution, in solemn council, to unseal the last will and testament of the Fathers—lay hold of their birthright of freedom, and keep it a sacred trust for all coming generations.

★ Susie King Taylor ★
STRANDED IN THE WOODS

The soldiers and civilians who lived through the Civil War had normal, day-to-day problems. In this excerpt from her autobiography, Susie King Taylor describes an embarrassing incident that happened when she was fifteen years old. She served as a nurse with the 33rd U.S. Colored Troops. After the war, Taylor went on to become a teacher and vocal advocate for war veterans of both sexes. She founded the Women's Relief Corps. This organization was made up of women who had worked alongside the Union armies during the war. She also compiled a list of Civil War veterans living in Massachusetts. This allowed many veterans to reestablish contact with others who had served in their regiments.

- **Susie King Taylor, *Reminiscences of My Life in Camp*. Boston: Taylor, 1902.**

I had rather an amusing experience; that is, it seems amusing now, as I look back, but at the time it occurred it was a most serious one to me. When our regiment left Beaufort for Seabrooke, I left some of my things with a neighbor who lived outside of the camp. After I had been at Seabrooke about a week, I decided to return to Camp Saxton and get them. So one morning, with Mary Shaw, a friend who was in the company at that time, I started off. There was no way for us to get to Beaufort other than to walk, except we rode on the commissary wagon. This we did, and reached Beaufort about one o'clock. We then had more than two miles to walk before reaching our old camp, and expected to be able to accomplish this and return in time to meet the wagon again by three o'clock that afternoon, and so be taken back. We failed to do this, however, for when we got to Beaufort the wagon was gone. We did not know what to do. I did not wish to remain overnight, neither did my friend, although we might easily have stayed, as both had relatives in the town.

It was in the springtime, and the days were long, and as the sun looked so bright, we concluded to walk back, thinking we should reach camp before dark. So off we started on our ten-mile tramp. We had not gone many miles, however, before we were all tired out and began to regret our undertaking. The sun was getting low, and we grew more frightened, fearful of meeting some animal or of treading on a snake on our way. We did not meet a person, and we were frightened almost to death. Our feet were so sore we could hardly walk. Finally we took off our shoes and tried walking in our stocking feet, but this made them worse. We had gone about six miles when night overtook us.

GLOSSARY

- **commissary wagon:** supply wagon
- **countersign:** password

This photo shows the typical Civil War camp in which volunteer nurses cared for wounded soldiers. The pictured camp's nurses are seated near the tent's entrance.

There we were, nothing around us but dense woods, and as there was no house or any place to stop at, there was nothing for us to do but continue on. We were afraid to speak to each other.

Meantime at the camp, seeing no signs of us by dusk, they concluded we had decided to remain over until next day, and so had no idea of our plight. Imagine their surprise when we reached camp about eleven P.M. The guard challenged us, "Who comes there?" My answer was, "A friend without a countersign." He approached and saw who it was, reported, and we were admitted into the lines. They had the joke on us that night, and for a long time after would tease us; and sometimes some of the men who were on guard that night would call us deserters. They used to laugh at us, but we joined with them too, especially when we would tell them our experience on our way to camp. I did not undertake that trip again.

★ Maria Isabella Johnson ★
THE CAVES OF VICKSBURG

For two months, residents of Vicksburg, Mississippi, were bombarded by invading Union forces. People took shelter in caves as Confederate forces attempted to hold off the Union assault. In this excerpt from her book on the siege of Vicksburg, Maria Isabella Johnson describes what these caves were like. On July 4, 1863, Confederate forces surrendered. The Union then took control of Vicksburg.

• **Maria Isabella Johnson, *The Siege of Vicksburg.* 1869.**

Since the place had been garrisoned, this street, usually so quiet, presented numerous signs of camp life. At the corner, below the house, a trench had been dug to hold sharp-shooters, in case the enemy should attempt to storm. Small pieces of cannon were arranged to command the declivity which sloped to the river-bank, and all the streets of the town being fixed in the same manner, and stronger fortifications placed on the bank and surrounding hills. . . .

Most of the caves that the frightened citizens of Vicksburg were scooping in the surrounding hills, were just large enough to admit a small mattress, on which the family, be it large or small, huddled up together, in a way that was injurious alike to comfort and health. A neighbor of Mr. Andrews's, however (an eccentric man), had taken a fancy, without any particular reason, to make for a favorite daughter one that . . . consisted of a hall, through which ran a line of earthen columns, opening into four chambers, containing furniture for bedrooms, dining-room, and parlor. The young lady's piano, books, and hot-house flowers were transported from his residence to ornament it; lamps were hung from the ceiling, burning all hours of the day and night; and nothing was left undone to make the damp, close air seem wholesome and cheerful, or to reconcile his darling to this subterranean retreat, which he deemed necessary to the pre-servation of her life.

Mr. Andrews had also been anxious to provide for the comfort of his family; but he doubted the sagacity of making excavations on so large a scale. An examination of the character of the soil made him fearful that thus undermining the bottom of the hill might make the top, particularly after the constant report of cannon began to jar it, cave in. He therefore contented himself with a much more moderate apartment, but one large enough to contain a good-sized bed and several chairs.

GLOSSARY

- **garrisoned:** fortified with troops
- **declivity:** incline
- **admit:** hold
- **injurious:** hurtful
- **eccentric:** slightly odd
- **reconcile:** to make compatible
- **subterranean:** underground
- **sagacity:** wisdom

An old Civil War photo shows the many caves in which Vicksburg, Mississippi, residents took shelter during the 1863 siege by Union forces.

★ Eliza Frances Andrews ★
THE BURNT COUNTRY

To destroy Confederate morale and supply lines, Union general William T. Sherman took the Civil War to Georgia's civilians for the last three months of 1864 in his "March to the Sea." Beginning in Atlanta, which he conquered in September, he marched east to Savannah. The Union troops left a path of destruction and famine behind them. Documenting this was "Fanny" Andrews, a college-educated native of Georgia. While on the way to visit her sister in Savannah (a visit that was cut short by Sherman's march), Andrews encountered the horribly desolate conditions left in the wake of the Union attacks. After the war, Andrews had a successful career as a novelist (under the pen name "Elzey Hay"), journalist, editor, and botanist.

- **Eliza Frances Andrews, *The War-Time Journal of a Georgia Girl.* New York: Appleton, 1908.**

A bout three miles from Sparta we struck the "Burnt Country," as it is well named by the natives, and then I could better understand the wrath and desperation of these poor people. . . . There was hardly a fence left standing all the way from Sparta to Gordon. The fields were trampled down and the road was lined with carcasses of horses, hogs, and cattle that the invaders, unable either to consume or to carry away with them, had wantonly shot down to starve out the people and prevent them from making their crops. The stench in some places was unbearable; every few hundred yards we had to hold our noses or stop them with the cologne Mrs. Elzey had given us, and it proved a great boon. The dwellings that were standing all showed signs of pillage, and on every plantation we saw the charred remains of the gin-house and packing-screw, while here and there, lone chimney-stacks, "Sherman's Sentinels," told of homes laid in ashes. The infamous wretches! I couldn't wonder now that these poor people should want to put a rope round the neck of every red-handed "devil of them" they could lay their hands on. Hay ricks and fodder stacks were demolished, corn cribs were empty, and every bale of cotton that could be found was burnt by the savages. I saw no grain of any sort, except little patches they had spilled when feeding their horses and which there was not even a chicken left in the country to eat. A bag of oats might have lain anywhere along the road without danger from the beasts of the field, though I cannot say it would have been safe from the assaults of hungry man.

Crowds of soldiers were tramping over the road in both directions; it was like traveling through the streets of a populous town all day. They were mostly on foot, and I saw numbers seated on the roadside

GLOSSARY

- **carcasses:** dead bodies
- **wantonly:** without purpose
- **boon:** benefit
- **pillage:** robbery, looting
- **infamous:** shamefully bad
- **provision:** food
- **prudence:** caution

As this photo grimly shows, very little remained after Gen. William T. Sherman's Union troops laid waste Georgia's cities and countryside in Sherman's 1864 "March to the Sea."

greedily eating raw turnips, meat skins, parched corn—anything they could find, even picking up the loose grains that Sherman's horses had left. I felt tempted to stop and empty the contents of our provision baskets into their laps, but the dreadful accounts that were given of the state of the country before us, made prudence get the better of our generosity.

★ *Rachel Bowman Cormany* ★

THE BURNING OF CHAMBERSBURG

Confederate general Jubal Early failed to lead a successful attack on Washington in July 1864. He reacted by ordering his troops to destroy vast amounts of civilian property in Pennsylvania. This was an attempt to weaken Northern support for the war. Early hoped to bring the war to a close without dissolving the Confederacy. One of his targets was the small town of Chambersburg. Rachel Cormany's husband, Samuel, was a soldier in the Union army. While staying with family in Chambersburg, she witnessed firsthand the horrors of Early's civilian attacks. When the town was unable to pay a high ransom, Confederate troops marched in and burned the city down.

- **John C. Mohr, ed., *The Cormany Diaries: A Northern Family in the Civil War.* Pittsburgh: University of Pittsburgh Press, 1982.**

This photo shows the near-total destruction of Chambersburg, Pennsylvania, by Confederate troops in 1864.

> ## GLOSSARY
> - **in default of which:** if it could not be paid
> - **rebs:** rebels (Confederates)
> - **fired:** set on fire
> - **considerable:** a lot

Just a week this morning the rebels turned up in our devoted town again. Before they entered they roused us out of our slumbers by throwing two shells in. This was between 3 and 4 A.M. By 5—the gray back hordes came pouring in. They demanded 500,000 dollars in default of which the town would be burned—They were told that it was impossible to raise that amount—The rebs then came down to 100,000 in gold which was just as impossible. When they were informed of the impossibility they deliberately went from house to house & fired it. The whole heart of the town is burned. They gave no time for people to get any thing out. Each had to escape for life & took only what they could first grab. Some saved considerable. Others only the clothes on their backs—& even some of those were taken off as they escaped from their burning dwellings. O! the 30th July 1864 was a sad day to the people of Chambersburg. In most of cases where the buildings were left money was paid. They were here too but we talked them out of it. We told them we were widows & that saved us here. About 3000 were made homeless in less than three hours. This whole week has been one of great excitement. We live in constant dread. I never spent such days as these few last I never spent—I feel as if I could not stay in this country longer. I feel quite sick of the dread & excitement.

FOR FURTHER READING

Books

James R. Arnold and Roberta Wiener, *Life Goes On: The Civil War at Home, 1861–1865*. Minneapolis: Lerner, 2003. Discusses the problems families faced during the Civil War.

Peggy Caravantes, *Petticoat Spies: Six Women Spies of the Civil War*. Greensboro, NC: Morgan Reynolds, 2002. Short (fifteen-page) biographies of the six best-known women spies of the Civil War, including Belle Boyd.

Duane Damon, *Growing Up in the Civil War, 1860 to 1864*. Minneapolis: Lerner, 2003. A collective biography of children who grew up during the Civil War, and the unique challenges they and their families faced.

Robert B. Noyed and Cynthia Fitterer Klingel, *Clara Barton: Founder of the American Red Cross*. Chanhassen, MN: Child's World, 2002. A detailed biography of Civil War nurse Clara Barton, who later founded the American Red Cross.

Douglas J. Savage, *Women in the Civil War*. Bloomall, PA: Chelsea House, 2000. A general overview of the role women played in the Civil War. Addresses nurses, abolitionists, and suffragists.

Websites

The American Civil War Homepage
sunsite.utk.edu/civil-war The largest general online directory of Civil War resources, maintained by Dr. George H. Hoemann of the University of Tennessee.

Women of the American Civil War
americancivilwar.com/women/women.html Short, readable biographies of women who played a prominent role in the Civil War.

INDEX